Cornel West

by Corinne J. Naden and Rose Blue

Raintree

Chicago, Illinois

Photo Research: Scott Braut

Printed and bound in China by South China Printing Company.
10 09 08 07 06
10 9 8 7 6 5 4 3 2 1

Library of Congress Cataloging-in-Publication Data:

Naden, Corinne J.
  Cornel West / Corinne J. Naden and Rose Blue.
     p. cm.
  Includes bibliographical references (p.   ) and index.
  ISBN 1-4109-1040-7 (hc) 1-4109-1124-1 (pb)
  1. West, Cornel--Juvenile literature. 2. African Americans--Biography--Juvenile literature. 3. African American intellectuals--Biography--Juvenile literature. 4. African American scholars--Biography--Juvenile literature. 5. African American college teachers--Biography--Juvenile literature. 6. African Americans--Social conditions--1975---Juvenile literature. 7. United States--Race relations--Juvenile literature. I. Blue, Rose. II. Title.
  E185.97.W56N33 2005
  305.896'073'0092--dc22

2005005118

Acknowledgments
The publisher would like to thank the following for permission to reproduce photographs:
p. 4 Richard B. Levine/Newscom; p. 6 Lonny Shavelson/Zuma/Corbis; p. 8 Library of Congress; pp. 10, 13, 15, 17, 20, 22, 24, 31, 46, 50 Bettman/Corbis; p. 28 Jeffrey Rothstein/The Image Works; p. 33 Michael Quan/Zuma Press/Newscom; p. 36 James Leynse/Corbis; p. 38 Lynsey Addario/AP Wide World Photo; p. 42 Neal Preston/Corbis; p. 44 Arnold Turner/WireImage.com; p. 52 Keith Meyers/New York Times; p. 56 Brian Branch-Price/AP Wide World Photo; p. 58 Scott Gries/Getty Images

Cover photograph: Richard B. Levine/Newscom

Every effort has been made to contact copyright holders of any material reproduced in this book. Any omissions will be rectified in subsequent printings if notice is given to the publisher

Some words are shown in bold, **like this**. You can find out what they mean by looking in the Glossary.

Contents

Professor Cornel West believes each person has the power to make the world a better place.

Introduction:
A Modern Intellectual

Cornel West is a thinker. He writes and speaks about the way he thinks the world works, especially where relationships between people of different races are concerned. West grew up at a time when black people had to fight for the same rights and privileges white people have. He has experienced **racism** first-hand, and as a child was violently angry about it. But as an adult, West refuses to hate anyone. He refers to anyone and everyone as his brother or sister. He believes each person is unique, wonderful, and full of the power to make the world a better place.

Cornel West is a professor of religion and African American studies at Princeton University. He is considered one of America's modern **intellectuals**. His work is taken seriously in the **academic** world. But he also tries hard to get his message out to people who might not read his books or attend his classes. He often speaks of life in terms of music and is very aware of what

Cornel West keeps his audiences captivated with the intelligence of his ideas, the pattern of his speech, and his expressive gestures.

young people like. He counts many rappers and hip-hop artists among his friends. He has also recorded two CDs of his own.

Not everyone agrees with West's message or the ways he chooses to deliver it, but he welcomes their criticism. In fact, he thinks it's important for everyone to be critical of the world around them. The only way to find out the truth about things, West believes, is to ask questions. West is always asking questions himself, and striving every day to find the answers.

In His Own Words

My concern has always been just trying to make sense of the world and trying to leave the world a little better than when I found it.

Tulsa Oklahoma as it looked in in the 1950s when Cornel was a young boy.

Chapter 1:
Unconditional Love

Cornel Ronald West was born on June 2, 1953 in Tulsa, Oklahoma. His father worked for the air force, so the family moved around a lot. In 1958, when Cornel was four years old, the family settled in a **segregated** section of Sacramento, California. For many years, Cornel grew up around only black people and black culture–his whole world was black. He didn't have the sense that white people were bad, like people a generation before had. White people had not come into his neighborhood and made him feel bad about being black. So by the time he went to school with white students in middle school, he just saw them as human beings.

Cornel's parents had grown up in the South, and had experienced first-hand the horrors of **racism**. In the South, blacks were not allowed to eat in the same restaurants as whites, were forced to use different bathrooms and drinking fountains, and black and white children attended separate schools. The drinking

This sign shows how segregated even every day life was in the South.

fountains, bathrooms, and schools that black people used were often dirty and run-down. They were not as good as the schools, drinking fountains, and bathrooms whites used. There were some white people who wanted things to stay this way. They did everything they could to keep black people from getting the rights and fair treatment they deserved. Some groups, like the Ku Klux Klan, attacked and murdered black people who tried to protest the way they were treated.

Even though they were afraid, blacks in the South still marched and protested. Many of the protests were successful, such as the 1955 bus boycott in Montgomery, Alabama. In Montgomery, and other cities across the South, Black people were forced to sit at the backs of buses. When the buses were crowded, they were forced to stand so that white passengers could sit down. In 1955 Rosa Parks refused to give up her seat to a white passenger. The bus driver called the police, and Parks was arrested. Her arrest inspired black people in Montgomery to stop riding the buses. For over a year, they walked to work. The bus companies lost money and eventually, the Supreme Court, the most powerful court in the United States, declared that **segregated** buses were illegal.

By the time Cornel was a young boy, many of the major fights for civil rights had been fought, but their effects came about slowly. Cornel's family made sure he understood what they were about. When he was 10 years old, they took him to a protest to give him a sense of history. They always made sure he understood that seven generations of his family had been slaves.

Cornel's family was very important to him when he was growing up–and still is. His mother, Irene West, was an elementary school teacher and principal. She was so well respected, that a school in Sacramento was named after her.

Grandfather West

Growing up, Cornel was extremely close to his grandfather, C. L. West. C.L. was a minister in Tulsa. He began his church with three people in his basement. Eventually, the church had 3,000 people. Cornel knew that his grandfather loved the members of his church–it's what made him such a good minister. But he knew that his grandfather put no one above his family.

Cornel's grandfather liked to tell stories. He would tell one about Cornel's christening (a naming ceremony that happens in a church). During the ceremony, something made the church members lose control and begin to sway. Then they broke into song. They sang about how special Cornel was and that God was watching him.

When Cornel was 10, his grandfather brought him in front of the church members again. He told his church that Cornel was going to change the world.

The person Cornel felt closest to in his family was his brother, Clifton L. West III. Even as an adult, Cornel counts Clifton as one of his heroes and considers his brother the true genius of the family. Cornel has said he hopes to someday be "half the man my brother is."

*In the 1950s **civil rights** protests began to become more common.*

Cornel has said that the greatest gift his parents gave him was unconditional love. They showed him how important it is to share that love with others—no matter who they are. This is probably why today Cornel refers to everyone as "brother" or "sister," even people he doesn't agree with. His parents also encouraged his curiosity about the world, and always reminded him that they believed love can change the world.

A first protest

Even surrounded by all this love, as a young boy Cornel had an angry streak. He doesn't know where it came from, but he remembers being filled, at times, with "anger and energy." At school, he had fights five to six times a week.

Among the stories his family told were stories about Cornel's relatives who fought in World War I. At that time, many places in the United States were extremely dangerous for black people. They were hated and sometimes attacked by **racist** white groups, especially in the South. Even though Cornel's relatives had fought to protect the United States in the war, they were attacked by some of these racist groups. Some of Cornel's relatives were shot while wearing their army uniforms. Others were hanged with the American flag.

This photo from the 1930s shows an early civil rights protest. The protest is a reaction to a crime conference's failure to acknowledge lynchings as a problem.

In third grade, when Cornel's teacher asked him to say the Pledge of Allegiance to the American Flag, he remembered these stories about how his relatives had been treated. He didn't want to salute the flag. His teacher slapped him for disobeying her and Cornel punched her in the stomach. He was then suspended from school and his mother taught him at home.

At about this time, Cornel discovered a book about Theodore Roosevelt, the 26th President of the United States. Reading the book, Cornel learned that Roosevelt had asthma, an illness that makes it difficult to breathe. Cornel had asthma, too. Roosevelt didn't let his asthma stop him from becoming president, and Cornel decided he wouldn't let his asthma stop him either. Roosevelt had gone to college at Harvard University. Even though he had never heard of Harvard before, Cornel decided that he would go there, too.

Because of his behavior, Cornel had a hard time getting into a new school. Finally, after six months of being taught by his mother, he enrolled in an **integrated** school across town. This was the first time Cornel went to school with white children. Cornel could tell there was something different about them. They had a different way of speaking, of dressing, listened to different music, and Cornel was very curious about them.

The writings of Danish author Kierkegaard had a strong influence on Cornel West.

High school

When Cornel was 13, he attended John F. Kennedy High School. He became a very serious student, wanting to "read and write the way James Brown danced and the way Aretha Franklin sang." He started reading the works of Danish writer and philosopher Søren Kierkegaard. From an early age, Cornel had realized that life had a sad side and that many people lived in fear. He thought that Kierkegaard, who wrote books with such titles as *Fear and Trembling*, *The Concept of Dread* and *Sickness Until Death* understood life's dark side.

The Black Panther Party

The Black Panther Party was formed in 1966 by Huey Newton and Bobby Seale. The group started in Oakland, California, but soon had members all over the country.

At the time, the **Civil Rights Movement** was in full-swing, led by Dr. Martin Luther King Jr. For years, King and others had led protests and marches to draw attention to mistreatment. Slowly but surely, the Civil Rights Movement was helping guarantee that African Americans were treated with the respect and dignity every American deserved. Although the protests King and others lead were peaceful, the police would sometime turn hoses on the protesters or beat them with their night sticks. Onlookers would join in the attacks. King taught his followers not to react to this violence. He believed that when attacked, African Americans should not fight back.

The Black Panther Party believed differently. They also wanted to change the way African Americans were treated. They promoted the idea that black people were beautiful. They wanted black people to gain power by owning their own businesses. But when they were attacked, especially by the police, members of the Black Panther Party fought back.

In the 1970s, after a tragic run-in with the Federal Bureau of Investigation (FBI) in which several key members of the Black Panther Party were killed, the organization softened a bit. Newton established several service programs in black communities nationwide, including a free breakfast program that Cornel West participated in. By the end of the 1970s, the Black Panther Party was no longer the powerful force it had once been.

Cornel wanted to find a way to lift himself and others out of the darkness. While in high school, he became very religious, which helped him overcome his mysterious anger. He also became involved in the **Civil Rights** Movement that was just beginning to take hold in the United States.

An organization called The Black Panther Party had an office not far from where Cornel went to church. The Black Panther Party was a group that believed in the power and strength of black people. They thought that African Americans should do whatever it took to be secure. Cornel did not agree with the Panthers' use of violence, but he did believe in some of the ideas the Panthers held dear. He became involved with some of the Black Panther community programs, but when he realized that the Panthers did not support his religious views, he left the group.

While in high school, Cornel had a brush with **racism** that stayed with him for the rest of his life. Cornel's track coach—a white man—wanted to teach him how to swim. The coach took Cornel to his all-white apartment complex where he had a pool. When Cornel jumped into the water, all the people who had been in the pool jumped out. Later, the pool was drained, simply because Cornel, a black boy, had been in it.

At this funeral of a Black Panther leader, mourners give the Black Panther, or Black Power, salute.

Despite the challenges, Cornel did well in high school. He became student body president and worked hard to bring the black and white students at John F. Kennedy High School together. Cornel took a cue from Dr. Martin Luther King Jr. King had a message of nonviolent unity among all people. Cornel felt King was the true hero of the **Civil Rights Movement**. Cornel participated in a number of student protests. In one case, with black student body presidents from other schools, he demanded that black history be taught in schools. The demonstration was not successful, but it was the beginning of his own career as an activist.

When Cornel graduated from high school in 1970, he earned a scholarship to Harvard University. Following in Theodore Roosevelt's footsteps, West enrolled at Harvard in the the fall of that year.

In this 1972 press conference members of Harvard's Pan African Liberation Committee explain why they have taken over offices at Harvard.

Chapter 2:
On Campus

Cornel West arrived at Harvard University knowing he was very lucky to be there. Harvard had once been a school for white students only. West understood that he was only able to attend Harvard because of all the protests and sacrifices generations of black people had made. He was one of only 96 black students in his class. The graduating class ahead of him had contained only 14 black students.

Wanting to understand how he fit into the world around him, Cornel decided to study history and **culture**. However, he soon switched his major to the study of languages from long ago.

At Harvard, West worked hard. At six o'clock each morning, he helped out with a program that provided breakfast for young kids who couldn't afford it. He visited with prisoners at the state prison in Norfolk, Virginia. He participated in protests lead by Harvard's

Protests like this were common at Harvard in the 1970s.

Pan African Liberation Committee. The most memorable of these protests happened in 1972. Members of the organization took control of the main campus building to show that they did not support some of Harvard's policies regarding countries in other parts of the world.

And of course, West spent a great deal of time studying and thinking about what he learned. He did well and impressed his teachers, but he also made time to have a little fun. He went to parties every weekend, and was known for doing a dance called a the "funky chicken."

During his sophomore year, West and two of his roommates—who were also black—were accused of attacking a white student who lived next door to them. The police officers who arrested them tried to convince the woman that West and his roommates were the ones who attacked her, but she told the officers that West and his friends were innocent. If this woman had not convinced the police, West is certain that he and his friends would have been sent to prison. In a later interview he said, "It was that moment that reminded me how much race does matter in our society."

Junior year was also a challenging one for West. He was running out of money and his parents couldn't afford to help. West took extra classes so he could graduate early. He also worked several jobs including cleaning toilets, washing dishes, and working as a

A respected leader

W.E.B. DuBois was a famous African-American in the first half of the 20th century. He was born in Massachusetts in 1868 and graduated from Fisk University, a black college in Nashville, Tennessee, in 1888. In 1895, he earned a doctorate degree from Harvard University.

From the beginning of his career, DuBois began asking questions about the condition of black people in the United States. Over the years, he wrote many articles that were published by Atlanta University. He was a professor there between 1897 and 1910. His book, *The Philadelphia Negro; A Social Study*, published in 1899, was the first case study of an African-American community in the nation.

In his early years, DuBois felt that study and knowledge could solve the race problem. But gradually he came to believe that **racism** could not be ended except by action and protest. This put him against many other black leaders in the country at the time. He especially disagreed with Booker T. Washington, who felt that blacks could change the race issue through hard work and making more money. DuBois's book *The Souls of Black Folk* (1903) attacked Washington's approach. It divided the black leadership community into two sides.

DuBois helped to found the Niagara Movement in 1905. The organization never grew in importance, but it sparked the National Association for the Advancement of Colored People (NAACP), which was founded in 1909. DuBois was a large part of its creation. As such, he was probably the most influential black leader in the country at that time.

mailman. He graduated from Harvard in 1973, with highest honors.

At age 19, West went to Princeton to get a master's degree in philosophy. While there, he began to think about how he wanted to live his life. He always knew how important it is to celebrate each person, no matter who he or she is, as a worthwhile individual, but now he really tried to figure out how get this message out to as many people as possible. He began to realize that the poorest and most needy people were often ignored by the government. He thought these people should get the same attention that people with money and power get. He began to think about helping to create a government that would do just that.

In 1975, after two years at Princeton, West earned his master's degree. That same year, Harvard announced the beginning of the W.E.B. Du Bois Institute of African and Afro-American Research. West returned to Harvard to study philosophy for another two years. While there, he got married and had a son, Clifton.

Cornel West as a young teacher.

Chapter 3:
Becoming a Teacher

In 1977, at the age of 24, West began his first full-time teaching job. He took a position as an assistant professor of religion at the Union Theological Seminary in New York City. A theological seminary is a school for religious study.

While at the seminary, West gave speeches in local churches. He wasn't a minister or preacher, but people who heard him speak thought he sounded a bit like one. West's grandfather and the other preachers he had known as a boy clearly influenced his passionate speaking style and attitude of love. For the next twenty years, West would give 150 speeches a year.

West spent seven years teaching at Union Theological Seminary. During that time, he went back to Princeton and completed his Ph.D. in philosophy. In 1984, he left Union to teach at Yale University's Divinity School in New Haven, Connecticut.

Yale

While at Yale, West participated in two protests that got him into trouble. One was in support of people who worked at Yale who weren't being paid enough money. The other was to express his disapproval of Yale's decision to support businesses in South Africa.

At the time, South Africa had a system of government called apartheid. Under apartheid, the black South Africans were treated much like African-Americans had been treated in the South when West's parents were growing up. They had few rights and most lived in poverty. The South African government was controlled by white people who did not want to see things change. But much like the African Americans in the South had in the 1950s, black South Africans were fighting to make their lives better.

West's participation in these protests lead to his arrest. He was sent to jail. He was the first professor at Yale ever to be arrested on campus. Rather than be embarrassed about his arrest, West was proud. He later wrote that he was pleased to show his son the importance of standing up for what you believe in, no matter what the cost.

Before his arrest, West had planned to take the spring 1987 term off so he could teach classes at the University of Paris in Paris, France. But because of his arrest, Yale would not allow him to take the time off. West taught at the University of Paris anyway.

In the 1980s students and professors across the country participated in demonstrations like this to protest universities that had money invested in South Africa. This protest is being held in Colorado. West was arrested at a similar protest at Yale.

From February to April, he flew between Paris and New Haven, teaching a full load of classes. On Monday mornings, he would teach two classes at Yale. On Thursdays and Fridays he would teach three classes at the University of Paris.

West was amazed by his French students. They were so hungry for any information about African-American history and culture. One of his classes was meant for only 20 students, but over 100 students signed up.

Going back and forth between the University of Paris and Yale got to be too much for West. He left both teaching positions and returned to Union in New York to teach. He was there only a year before author Toni Morrison convinced him to join her at Princeton. There he became a professor of religion and the head of Princeton's African-American studies program. He stayed at Princeton for five years.

While teaching at Yale, West met Ellani Gabre Amlack, a woman from Ethiopia. Ethiopia is a country in northeastern Africa. West and Amlack got married in 1992 in Addis Ababa, the capital city of Ethiopia. The couple spends nearly every summer there in a home once owned by Amalack's mother.

Henry Louis Gates Jr. is the head of the African American Studies department at Harvard. He is interested in many race-related issues, but is focused on the importance of African-American literature.

Race Matters

In his book *Race Matters*, published in 1993 West discusses leaders such as Martin Luther King Jr., and Fannie Lou Hamer. King (1929–1968) was a Baptist minister who led a generation, black and white, into a nonviolent fight for **civil rights**. He was born in Atlanta, Georgia, and attended Morehouse College under a special program for gifted students. As the leader of the Southern Christian Leadership Conference (SCLC), he led nonviolent protests throughout the country in the 1950s and 1960s. He was assassinated in Memphis, Tennessee. King was awarded the **Nobel Prize** for Peace in 1964, and a national holiday is observed in his honor on the third Monday in January.

Fannie Lou Hamer (1917–1997) was born in Mississippi, the granddaughter of a slave. One of 20 children, her parents were **sharecroppers**. She was six years old when she began helping out in the cotton fields, and had to drop out of school to work. She later married another sharecropper, Perry Hamer. But in 1962, she decided that she had had enough of sharecropping. So she took a bus with other sharecroppers to register to vote. She was refused because the police said the bus she was riding in was the wrong color and she went to jail.

When she returned home, the landowner kicked her off the land for making trouble, even though she had been there for 18 years. She and her husband went to live with another family.

Fannie Lou Hamer started to work for SCLC. In 1963, she and other civil rights workers were beaten, and she nearly lost the sight in one eye. But she would not back down. She worked on the 1964 presidential election for the newly created Mississippi Freedom Democratic Party (MFDP). The new party challenged the all-white Democratic party in Mississippi. The following year, President Lyndon B. Johnson signed the Voting Rights Act that outlawed **discrimination** in voting.

A teacher at Harvard

By now, West had published three books about how people of different races got along in the United States. He had a powerful reputation as a brilliant man with lots to say. In 1994 Henry Louis Gates, a well-known black professor at Harvard, wanted to bring West's brilliance back to Harvard. Gates was putting together a group of top African-American thinkers to create what he hoped would be the best African-American studies department in the world. He wanted West to be part of his team. At first West didn't want to be part of Gates' project, but when he learned of the other great thinkers who would be involved, West changed his mind.

The Million Man March

While West was at Harvard, problems facing some African Americans, such as poverty, violence, and poor educational opportunities were getting a lot of attention. Some black leaders were especially concerned about African American men and thought it was time black men came together to figure out how to make their lives better.

To address these concerns, Minister Louis Farrakhan organized what came to be known as the Million Man March. It was an invitation for a million black men to unite and pledge to improve their lives. It was modeled after the march Dr. Martin Luther King Jr. had organized in Washington thirty years earlier.

Cornel West has publicly spoken out against Louis Farrakhan (seen here at the Million Man March), but he has also said that it is important to see Farrakhan as "a human being who is concerned about suffering."

Minister Farrakhan is the leader of the Nation of Islam, a group that believes that African Americans are strong and powerful even though they have historically not been treated well in the United States.

Not everyone agrees with Louis Farrakhan and the things he believes. He has said negative things about different **cultures**, especially Jewish people, that have made some people see him as dangerous. But many people liked the idea of bringing a million black men together in a positive way. Even people who disagreed with Farrakhan came out to support the Million Man March, including Cornel West. West's appearance at the march on October 16, 1995 drew a lot of criticism. But West thought that being part of the march was important. He thought it would be a great way for black men to learn to trust and respect one another.

Trouble at Harvard

For seven years, things went smoothly for West at Harvard. Then, in 2001, Harvard got a new president. By the time Lawrence H. Summers arrived on campus, West was making quite a name for himself. He was not just a popular professor who spoke to large numbers of students. Since the publication of his book, *Race Matters*, he was also an increasingly well-known writer, especially about race relations. He was a very popular speaker at college campuses all over the country.

Here West has a chat with Rev. Al Sharpton. West sees Sharpton as a leader willing to take risks to do what he considers the right thing.

Soon after he took office, Summers called a meeting with West. According to West, Summers told West he thought West was spending too much time away from Harvard doing things other than teaching. He accused West of missing too many classes. According to other reports, Summers also accused West of grade inflation. This means he thought West gave students high grades the students did not really deserve.

At the time, West was helping Al Sharpton with his campaign for president of the United States. Sharpton had been involved in the fight for **civil rights** for many years. He saw himself as the one presidential candidate who would pay attention to the needs of poor people and minority groups, such as Hispanics and African Americans. When he learned that Summers had criticized West for being involved in the campaign, Sharpton demanded a meeting with the universiy president.

Summers also thought West's interest in making music was inappropriate for a Harvard University professor. In 2002, West released a CD called *Sketches of My **Culture***. He hoped the CD would reach people who were interested in his message but probably wouldn't read his books. *Sketches of My Culture* is part rap, part rhythm and blues, and full of messages of pride, hope, and understanding. Summers thought West should be spending his time outside the classroom writing important books.

Although the meeting between Summers and West was private, people soon found out about what the two men had discussed. In a radio interview, West said that he felt insulted and angry when he left the meeting with Summers.

While his disagreements with Summers continued, West was diagnosed with cancer. In January 2001, he had the cancerous tumor removed.

The aftermath

When news of the disagreement between the two men became known, other people spoke out against Summers. They accused him of not paying attention to the African-American studies program and of not supporting it. Henry Louis Gates and Kwame Appiah also got into the discussion with Summers.

Later, Summers and West had another meeting during which the president apologized for his earlier words. After that, he did not want to talk about the matter any longer. But the damage had already been done.

Rumors spread that Gates, West, and writer Kwame Appiah, another member of Harvard's African American Studies department would all be leaving Harvard and going to Princeton. However, after a long meeting with the president, Gates decided to remain. He believed that Summers would do all he could to strengthen and promote Harvard's black studies program. But Appiah and West had already made up their minds. Both of them decided to go back to Princeton.

Harvard University

Harvard University is located in Cambridge, Massachusetts, near Boston. Founded in 1636, Harvard is the oldest institution of higher learning in the United States. Originally, Harvard had nine students and one teacher. Today there are more than 18,000 students and more than 2,000 faculty members.

Seven former presidents of the United States went to Harvard, and it has long been known as one of the finest schools in the world. Harvard's system of "houses" marks it as different from other American colleges. At Harvard, students are divided into thirteen houses. Each house has its own dining area, library, social activities, and tutors assigned to it. Students live in the houses (there is one house for students who do not live on campus). Many students feel this system gives them both a sense of community and individualized attention.

The first African American student was admitted in 1865, and the first female student in 1943. Prior to 1943 women attended Harvard's "sister school," Radcliffe.

James Brown, known as the Godfather of Soul, is one of West's favorite performers.

Chapter 4:
The Importance of Music

West returned to Princeton University in 2002 as a professor of religion. The school was very happy to welcome him back. As for West himself, he said he was comfortable returning to Princeton where he felt that his ideas were respected.

Although West was back in his classroom and his office, he was still active in causes outside the classroom. In April 2002 West attended a protest meeting in Washington, D.C. He and other demonstrators were protesting U.S. policy in the Middle East. West was one of 20 arrested for **civil disobedience**. The jail sentence lasted about nine hours.

In the summer of 2002, West was invited by the singer and songwriter Prince to attend a weeklong music conference. Prince is known for blending rock and funk music styles. He asked West to the concert after hearing of West's interest in rap music. The concert was held in Prince's hometown of Minneapolis, Minnesota.

Cornel West, actress Angela Basset, and the musician Prince at the 2005 NAACP image awards.

Prince called it "Xenophobia," a word that means "fear or hatred of strangers."

A life long interest

West's interest in music began long before his participation in the Xenophobia concert or even the 2002 release of his CD. Music has been important to West throughout his life. He has said that music restores his soul. He even turned down a job at Harvard, at one point, because he didn't think Boston radio stations played enough black music. Even the way he dresses, in neat three-piece suits with a black scarf–is a nod to the cool jazz musicians of the past.

West believed that for African Americans, music is history. It has helped black people survive many hardships and struggles. Borrowing a line from African American poet LeRoi Jones (also known as Amiri Baraka), West thinks of African Americans as "blues people."

Singin' the Blues

What does it mean to be blues people? According to West, it means being able to face the darknes and still smile. "[Black people]," he says, "have a willingness–a courageous willingness–to look misery in the face and not allow it to have the last word, even if it's so overwhelming … that all we can do is sing a song, or pray a prayer, or preach a sermon, or smile, or be silent. It's not allowing that sorrow and suffering to have the last word. That's Black folk at our best."

While West thinks of blues as a way of handling what life throws your way, many people think of the blues as a kind of music that tells very sad stories. Blues can sometimes be funny, too. It's the kind of music people sing when they want to feel better about something that has upset them very much.

Saxophone player John Coltrane is one of West's personal heroes.

According to West, blues began with the emotional cries of the slaves, which, says West, can be heard in church music, in the wail of a blues player's saxophone and in the moan of a blues singer's voice. He believes that today, rap and hip-hop are part of this tradition. West likes the way some rap music talks about the pain of **racism** and poverty, but he doesn't like gangster rap's messages of violence and the mistreatment of women. All of this music, says West, is a way to keep the sadness away, to keep moving toward something better. It's also a way to stay connected to the past.

John Coltrane

West has said that the person he admires most in history is John Coltrane.

John William Coltrane was born on September 23, 1926, in Hamlet North Carolina. He learned to play the clarinet when he was 12, and at age 13, was playing alto saxophone. In 1943 Coltrane graduated from high school and enrolled in a music school in Philadelphia. Two years later, he joined the navy. He was stationed in Hawaii where he played saxophone in the navy band.

After two years with the navy, Coltrane returned to Philadelphia and began playing professionally. He switched from alto to tenor sax. Over the next few years, he played in band with famous musicians like jazz trumpeters Dizzy Gillespie and Miles Davis. While touring with Davis, Coltrane became world-famous himself.

In the 1960s, Coltrane formed his own band and began to develop his own style. He found ways to make unusual sounds, and sometimes his music was hard to understand.

Coltrane was a shy, soft-spoken man. He let his music speak for him. Sometimes he played solos that were twenty minutes long with so much energy, it was hard for other people to keep up.

Coltrane died in 1967 of liver cancer. In 1981, he was awarded a Grammy for his contributions to the world of music.

Coltrane spent his life trying to find his own form of musical expression. He truly succeeded with his 1964 masterpiece "A Love Supreme." Coltrane was known as a master improviser. This means that he made up the music as he played; it wasn't always written down. Coltrane wasn't afaid to take risks in his music, which is one reason West admires him. When you listen to "A Love Supreme," West once said in an interview, "you know this brother ... who played his horn 18 hours a day, went to sleep with the horn in his mouth and woke up blowing was disciplined."

Like West, Coltrane was a spiritual man. Making his music helped him understand the world. People who saw him play live often thought that he played as if he were under a spell; as if something very powerful beling his music. Some people called him "a holy man with a horn."

West also admires Coltrane because he used his music to speak out about the problems black people faced in the United States. His 1963 piece "Alabama" was a tribute to four African-American girls who were killed when members of the Ku Klux Klan bombed a church in Birmingham, Alabama.

Duke Ellington

Another artist West admires is Duke Ellington. Ellington was a famous composer, bandleader, and performer. He began performing jazz in the 1900s and eventually was responsible for showing Americans that jazz could be serious music.

Duke Ellington was born Edward Ellington in 1899. He began taking music lessons as a young boy. His friends gave him the nickname "Duke" because of his good manners. He formed his first band in 1917. Soon after, Duke moved to Harlem, New York. At this time many African American artists were moving to Harlem and a culture of pride in the African American tradition was born. This period is known as the Harlem Rennaisance.

Ellington died in 1974. He continued to be active in music and in changing music throughout his life.

For most of his life West has thought of things in terms of music. In 1975, while he was teaching at Harvard, West wrote a short story about a man who lost his hearing and could no longer

*Pianist Duke Ellington was one of the leading figures of the Harlem Rennaisance, an important time in African-American **culture**.*

enjoy the music he loved so much. Writing about the story later West said that it helped him discover how he wanted present his ideas to people. He wanted to "sing in spoken word and written texts like Duke Ellington plays and Sarah Vaughn [a famous jazz singer] sang—to swing, to create an intellectual performance that had a blues sensibility and jazz-like openness, to have the courage to be myself and find my voice."

In His Own Words

When I was an undergraduate at Harvard, I used to listen to James Brown every time I was about to take an exam, and it would fire me up... I'd walk right into my exam, ready.

Cornel West loves introducing new ideas to his students.

Chapter 5:
A Message for Young People

For all the work and writing he has done about the state of the world, Cornel West is worried. He doesn't think there are leaders out there who are willing to do what it takes to make the world a better place. He hopes that the next generation will be willing to make the changes that are needed.

To do this, West believes young people need to get excited about learning. He has taken it upon himself to try to reach young people in ways that matter to them. He has appeared in the highly popular *Matrix* movie sequels as the wise Counsellor West.

He is also trying to reach young people through music of his own. In 2004, West released what he calls "danceable education" –*Street Knowledge,* his second CD. He doesn't believe that listening to his CD will take the place of reading a book, but he hopes that his CDs, which contain lessons about Malcolm X and

Martin Luther King, Jr. will encourage young people to be respectful of each other rather than insulting. West hopes the CD will make his listeners think. "If you are reading a short story or novel, or history," says West, "or if you are listening to some good music, this expands you. It deepens you. So as you listen and as you read, you have a deeper sense of the world."

Not everyone appreciates West's approach. Some see his work as superficial, or shallow.

Inspirational reading

With all of his focus on the importance of reading, what does West like to read? When asked, he named three works: *The Student* by Russian writer Anton Chekhov, *The Bluest Eye*, by Toni Morrison, and *The Fire Next Time*, by James Baldwin.

The Student is a short story about a young man who realizes that the present is linked to the past. Chekhov lived from 1860-1904. He began writing short stories in the late 1800s to support his family, and soon became known as one of the best writers in the world. West enjoys Chekhov because he wrote about real life in a way that everyone could understand. He has called Chekhov the "John Coltrane of modern drama."

The Bluest Eye, by Toni Morrison, is about a little girl who thinks no one loves her because she is black. She thinks that if she has blue eyes like her white doll has, everyone will love her. She wishes so hard for blue eyes that in the end, she goes insane. Toni Morrison was born in 1931. She began to write fiction when she was a student at Howard University, but she didn't publish any of her work until years later. Her first book was *The Bluest Eye*. West admires Morrison's writing because she tells the truth about hardships African Americans have suffered. She isn't afraid to describe them in horrible detail.

The Fire Next Time, by James Baldwin is a collection of essays. In them, Baldwin warned that if white people did not change their attitudes toward African Americans, black people would react violently. He did not want to see this happen, but he feared that it was already brewing. Baldwin lived from 1927–1987. He was a preacher at the age of 14 and grew up to write about **racism** in the United States. Of Baldwin, West has said, "He told the truth before it was fashionable."

A sense of history

Beyond having an appreciation for reading, West wants young people to have a sense of their history, to feel like they can connect with their past. One way to do that is to connect to the music of the past. He knows that young people are doing that on a certain level, because he believes rap and hip–hop are part of the African American musical traditon of protest music.

West is seen here leaving a juvenile detention center in New Jersey. In April 2005 West spoke to teens at the detention center urging them to remain true to themselves. West believes reaching out to all young people is important.

In 1997 West told an interviewer that while there were more famous, and prominent African Americans today than in the 1960s, in the 1960s average people had a better sense of community. He said that people were worse off in terms of things like money, but may have been better off in terms of **culture** and connection to others.

But for all his concern about knowledge and history, West believes that intelligence and book knowledge are less valuable than the protection of human life and the environment. He hopes that young people will come together to help make better lives for everyone.

In His Own Words

You really have to respect the world of young people, and I can't respect it without learning and becoming a part of it, though I can't ever fully become a part of it because I'm just older.

In 2001, Cornel West (Shown here with Russell Simmons and Lyor Cohen, the president of Def Jam Records) spoke at the Hip Hop Summit in New York City.

In His Own Words

I think that I am just a brother who comes out of the black church on the block, trying to make sense of the world, and making a blow for freedom in the short time that I'm here, and having fun in the meantime. I would also say that I'm one-half the person my brother is, and one-third the person my father was. I hope that I can actually... keep alive in some sense the depths of my mother and the determination of my sisters!

Glossary

academic pertaining to a school or university

brutality cruel or harsh act

civil disobedience charge given for such things as refusing to break up a protest demonstration when ordered by police

civil rights rights of all U.S. citizens to fair and equal treatment under the law

Civil Rights Movement name given to the long fight to gain civil rights for African Americans

culture lifestyle, feelings, religion, and actions of a group

discrimination pointing out differences based on such things as race or creed instead of individual merit

fellowship arrangement to study or teach at a university

influential quality of making a difference to someone

integrated mixing of differences, such as the races

intellectual person said to be guided by brain power rather than emotion

Nobel Prize any of various prizes in literature and other fields given through the will of Alfred Nobel

racism belief that one person is superior based only on race

racist person who dislikes another on account of race or creed

riot large uncontrolled fight involving a group

segregated keeping apart, as the races

sharecroppers those who live on and work the land that is owned by another

Timeline

1952   Cornel West born Tulsa, Oklahoma, on June 2.

1970   Enters Harvard University, Massachusetts.

1973   Graduates Harvard; enters Princeton University, New Jersey.

1974   Earns master's degree from Princeton; returns to Harvard under DuBois fellowship.

1973   Becomes assistant professor of religion, Union Theological Seminary, New York City.

1977   Earns doctor's degree from Princeton; joins Democratic Socialists of America.

1982   Publishes first book, *Prophecy Deliverance! An Afro-American Revolutionary Christianity*.

1984   Becomes associate professor at Union Theological Seminary; joins staff of Yale University, Connecticut; works as part-time reporter for *Le Monde Diplomatique*.

1989   Returns to Princeton to reorganize African-American studies program.

1990   Publishes *Prophetic Fragments*.

1991   Publishes *Breaking Bread*.

1993   Publishes *Race Matters*.

1994   Joins staff at Harvard.

1998   Publishes *The War Against Parents: What We Can Do for America's Beleaguered Moms and Dads*.

2001   Produces CD "Sketches of My Culture."

2002   Becomes professor of religion at Princeton; is arrested for civil disobedience demonstration, Washington.

Further Information

Further reading

Byers, Ann. *African-American History from Emancipation to Today.*
Berkeley Heights, NJ: Enslow, 2004.

Lester, Julius. *Let's Talk about Race.* New York: Harper, 2005.

Morrison, John. *Cornel West.* Philadelphia: Chelsea, 2004.

Myers, Walter D. *Malcolm X: By Any Means Necessary.*
New York: Scholastic,1993.

Address

Cornel R. West
Princeton University
Princeton, NJ 08544
cwest@princeton.edu

Index